Ciento: 100

100-Word

Love Poems

Other works by Lorna Dee Cervantes

Emplumada (1981)

American Book Award

From the Cables of Genocide:
Poems on Love and Hunger (1991)

Patterson Poetry Prize
Institute of Latin American Writers Poetry Prize
Latino Literature Award

DRIVE: The First Quartet (2006)

International Latino Book Award
Balcones Poetry Prize

Ciento: 100

100-Word

Love Poems

A amor, amar, amat
allí, allá, acá
por vida.

Lorna Dee Cervantes

WingsPress

San Antonio, Texas
2011

Ciento: 100 100-Word Love Poems
© 2011 by Wings Press, for Lorna Dee Cervantes

Front cover image: Photograph © 2008 by Pasquale Sorrentino. Used by
permission. Excavations near Mantua, Italy,
revealed the remains of a young man and woman
buried in an embrace, approximately 4,500 B.C. The
"lovers" were both less than 20 years of age.

First Wings Press Edition

Print edition ISBN: 978-0-916727-84-0
Ebook editions:
ePub ISBN: 978-1-60940-153-5
Kindle ISBN: 978-1-60940-154-2
Library PDF ISBN: 978-1-60940-155-9

Wings Press
627 E. Guenther
San Antonio, Texas 78210
Phone/fax: (210) 271-7805
On-line catalogue and ordering:www.wingspress.com
All Wings Press titles are distributed to the trade by
Independent Publishers Group
www.ipgbook.com

Library of Congress Cataloging in Publication Data:

Cervantes, Lorna Dee.
   Ciento : 100 100-word love poems : a amor, amar, amat allí, allá, acá por
vida / Lorna Dee Cervantes. -- 1st Wings Press ed.
      p. cm.
   ISBN 978-0-916727-84-0 (trade pbk., printed edition : alk. paper) --
ISBN 978-1-60940-153-5 (epub ebook) -- ISBN 978-1-60940-154-2
(kindle ebook) -- ISBN 978-1-60940-155-9 (library pdf ebook)
   1. Love poetry, American. I. Title. II. Title: Ciento : one hundred one
hundred-word love poems. III. Title: 100 100-word love poems. IV. Title:
100-word love poems. V. Title: One hundred one-hundred-word love poems.
VI. Title: One hundred word love poems.
   PS3553.E79C54 2011
   811'.54--dc22   2011023989

*For you and you and you and you
and even you, and always for You,
Dear Reader.*

In gratitude to my lovely and loving blog buddies;
You know who you are, and you know You.

Contents

I.

Possibilities—In 100 Words 3
100 Words Towards Possibility 4
100 Words to Spirit 5
100 Words For the Rehab of The Sea 6
Bound: 100 Words to You 7
Poem Where I Breathe 100 Words of You 8
100 Words to Radiant 9
100 Words & 9 Haiku Into The Distraction of You 10
100 Words Over How I Don't Bear A Grudge . . . 12
100 Words to Your Secrets 13
100 Words Out of Miscommunication 14
100 Torrid Words to Win You 15
100 Words On Being Done 16
Recherchê: 100 Words to the New 17
100 Words On Mistressing the Craft of You 18
100 Words On the Resourcefulness Of Loving You 19
100 Words On Loving the Latitudinarian You 20
100 Words to Please You 21
100 Words for Love's Restraint 22
100 Words for Wind 23

II.

100 Words, 100 Toys For You 27
100 Words to Your Grotto 28
100 Words To A Pixellated & Pixilated You 29
100 Words to Be Pixilated By You 30
100 Words to the Kalcidoscope of You 31
100 Words Out of Respect For You 32
100 Words In the Exact Moment of You 33

100 Words to A Distant You   34
100 Words Past Poverty   35
100 Words Against Poverty   36
100 Words For Neruda's Mercy   37
100 Words On My Blogging You   38
100 Words to the Scandal of You   39
100 Words to Your Feet   40
100 Wings to Your Ocean   41
100 Words to Your Blood   42
100 Words to Your Liquor   43
100 Words for My Ass   44
100 Words to the Poser You   45
100 Words After the Family of You   46

III.

100 Words For Fire   49
100 Words For Your Word: Kiss   50
100 Words to the Mystery of You   51
100 Words of Notice   52
100 Words to Fine   53
100 Words of Hope   54
I Am Ripening; Or, 100 Words For Your Release   55
100 Words to Nail You   56
100 Splendid Words For the Loneliness ...   57
100 Words On the Rock of You   58
100 Words of Restraint (an elegy)   59
100 Words For Change   60
100 Words to Receive You   61
100 words to Vibrate You   62
100 Words for Money   63
100 Words of Quiet, To You   64
100 Words for Provocative You   65
100 Words to the Perception of You   66

100 Words In Celebration of You 67
100 Words For A Fragmented You 68

IV.

100 Words From My Woolen Heart 71
100 Words Against the Gamma Ray You 72
100 Words Against the Aurora Borealis 73
100 Words Thankful For You 74
100 Words While I Wait 75
100 Words of Fantasy 76
100 Words For Queer Weather 77
100 Words to Illuminate You 78
100 Words of Goodbye 79
100 Words to Stimulate You 80
100 Word Vignette 81
100 Words In Kerfuffle 82
100 Words For the Impossible 83
100 Words to Repeat 84
100 Words For An Unknown 85
100 Words to the Genius of You 86
100 Words to a Noisy You 87
100 Words to Toast 88
100 Words to Unfold You 89
100 Words For Compass 90

V.

100 Words On How I Don't Aspire to You 93
100 Words to the Synchronicity of You 94
100 Words Against the Tether 95
100 Words to Content 96
100 Words to Your Organ 97
100 Words For You to Adapt 98

100 Words For Child   99
100 Words to the Chaos (Without You)   100
100 Words For A Star   101
100 Words to the Oddities of You   102
100 Words to Meander to You   103
100 Words For How I Don't Mind the Grunge   104
100 Words For Past Repast   105
100 Words For An Auspicious Beginning   106
100 Words to Google   107
100 Fresh Words   108
100 Words For Unforgettable You   109
100 Words For Depression   110
100 Words For Your Shelter   111
100 Words For You At Last   112

About the Author   115

I.

After I said I was going to "multiply the conditions
of possibility" and you said, "Okay. Good." I knew it
was the wrong answer to the wrong question. And
    afterwards,
every hummingbird was you. A murder of crows on my
elm tree became you finally calling my number, a slumber
of vultures circling my apartment, a single red fox roaming
my neighborhood, beat up, but there; a leftover garden
in a place someone is leaving: hard red pots left over
in the move. After I said, "I love you," you
could have hammered me over the heart with the silence.

Love is the possibility of doubting,
the possibility of making a mistake,
the possibility of searching and experimenting,
the possibility of saying "no" and whispering, "yes."

All the possibilities under your eyelids alight.
Aloft in your heart, a new timber for the flame,
a new car in which you are the key. All the possibilities
of you in a single line, a narrow column, filter

through the censors and commit.
All the possibilities in a drop of rain, a moment
of snow, a blank book by the fire—Love is
the possibility you'll wear it well, that new love smell.

Ask me again, where's my
spirit of adventure? I want
your heart in a basket,
a keg of you without
the glass. I'll be bubbles
up your thigh, the sighs
of millionaires and misers. I
want to express the sea
out of you, leave only
the rasp, a cat's tongue
licking up my armor. Try
and catch the silken touch,
the willing must, the rain.
Over and over again, winter,
with his hands on you,
your hair, your mussed-up
smile. Autumn doesn't deserve you.
Summer played all day, a
sheen of wet lather and
lust. Trust and thrust. Spirit.

I'm taking the sea in
for rehab. It seems she's
been crying into her crabmeat
and drinking the rain in
a seashell cup. She moans
with otters, moons sea lions
lying on the planks. Look
under the wharf and see
the sea passed out, vacant
and shining under setting Sun.
I'm gathering her former glory:
organdy dress of tides, tidy
surf at Sea's hem, her
humming on a summer's day.
I'm taking the bitch into
rehab—she is much too
in love with dumb Sun.
See her showing her locks
and her assets off? Seething.
Seething under ignorance;
and, love.

I was bound to love
you, bound by the possibilities
of you—the sea under
your stars, the long rehab
loving the lit bed of
your making, the way you
love those places of swell
and salt, thrust and gush.

I was bound to follow
your crumbs, the leftover pillars,
the awestruck wake. I'm bound
to travel across the length
of your languorous continent, bounding
through the map of you,
lost in the promise—wet
haze of your gaze; propelled

by what gazes back: you,
your Spirit-hardened heart; words
whipping into bindings; me, bound
to say it: transformed by you.

First time falling into you
I remember to breathe, breathe

your faint scent of sage,
soft coming of winter, summer's

sensuous leanings. First fall
moon, I look to you:

moon-face, sudden, luxuriously lugubrious and
brimming. And breathing in this

freedom, this horse sense, this
breaking at the gate, this

no bit flyer—my heart
in its stall—I linger

over autumn, and leave my
scent traced across your chest,

our kiss from the ancestors'
blessings, our ant trail following

us back home, warm, heartened.
Our breath locked in rhythms

of goddesses, taut codices: our
story waiting to be read.

You, in the radiant crepuscular
light, your succulent heart, sex-sucked
lips, your twining hair all
halo and sash, you fill
like the hummingbird—suckle, stay.

I am radiant to imagine
you: half animal, half staff
of ember, your lightening rays
of mirth, unimaginable in the dark,
in other than holding. You,
in a Spirit land, whisked
away to grace my hand.
The giving night, the airy
dawn, the awakening from withdrawal.
As the valley hunkers, mist
hangs around her love, River,
I flow with you, fog-struck
and caught in your aperture.
Your appetite for me, your
blessing kiss—eyes, whim-struck, radiant.

Your face—distraction
Distracting as a hickey
You me everywhere

Too darned many forms
Of you—earth air fire water
Your enormous sea

Opening into
Dawn this talking fast walking
Slow touching—silence

Tree limbs branching out
Each flowering memory
In hummingbird's dream

This autumn burning
You distract me—your fne smoke
From some ancient source

Cloud banks frost flies long
Red-Faced leaves—you leave me won
On some dream window

You your long rainbow
Of distraction—every hue
Anew—new world too

Eucalyptus pods
Serendipitously sweet
Sensitivities

Two windows / one world
Our passing through expands us
A distraction—you

I don't carry a grudge
against the government.
I have the nation of you.
I have your hands and
what they can do. I have
the heart of you—special
core of your purpose and
power. I have the gift
of your sweat stained sage,
your hummingbird's bliss,
sanctuary that you would find
in me. I don't carry
a grudge for any mortal. I
have the fire of you.
I don't bear a grudge for the stars,
the shifting planets,
sea's repel and contract, all
those contracts of amor,
broken and otherwise. I have
this treaty with the heart.

I'm sworn to the secrets
of you, sworn to secrecy
regarding your secret lust
for living, your giving ways,
the way you unroll me
like a packet of nickels.
Spend me to a dime.
Leave me, an expired ticket
to your floating show boat.
All the secrets in one
lonely face reveal the smile
you take, unveil the excruciating
detail of you—your leaving,
your twisted laugh, the dark
hair under your pink sigh.
All the trust in war
has nothing on your designs.
My desire for your touch
touches me in a place
I can never tell you.

Sure, it was a miscommunication
in spirit, an argument in
fact. We dried our eyes
of seas and wet seasons.
We expired and reinspired our
selves and licked the envelope
of our desires. We hashed
and remashed, replayed and played
again the tape of ages:
you, lost in an avenue
of abandonment; me, named Lost
at birth, my sooty streets
abandoned and haunted by men
frothing between their legs. It
was a miscommunication, the blacked
out nights of lazy heart,
the Limited that ran all
night through our enameled nightmares,
the fierce animals populating there,
our art of resistance: love.

Too torrid, you and I,
volcano meeting sun: reddening horizon
of our hips, the sweet
sucking of reed to flint,
the scent of summer melting
into slick. I was this
curling leaf, the second coming,
an unplayed instrument of torrid
catgut and wire. Unstrung. Undone.
Won. You woo me past
the wintering. I love you
past the withering. All this
passion for ice, for breaking,
for sharp words—a memory
folded into ash. I strip
you down to your shivering.
You suckle my skin into
blossoming. Tiny eruptions under my
heart spell it in braille.
Read me! Read Me! Read.

I'm done with demons; dying
by the dram. I'm done
with dealing diamonds from my
hand; done doubting the way
destiny pays; done doubling up
on trouble; done with debits
defining me, dollars dividing me;
done doing it up just
to have it undone; done
denying the outcome. I'm done.
I want bread and your red
arabesques on my neck. I
want the guards at my
borders to grant you entry.
I want to enter your
bed, lay down your arms,
speak you when spoken
to—I want to be
your native tongue, your native
touch, your single braid—undone.

I have to say: recherchê,
the way you move me,
sway me. Overblown faces gaze,
recherchê, their fates on fire.
But you, lyre, the music
you pump from me: recherchê,
uncommon, rare, this filling up,
this exquisite choice, this rate
we get from the exchange.
Recherchê, not the forced liking
of the unrefined, just you,
your way, your bushy canyons,
purple majesties between your thighs.
You express me, play me,
sing me into night. Dawn
doesn't do me without you.
Just you. Your recherchê recipes,
your truffles and your roe,
your salmon, leaping, has me,
spawning—a new word: you.

Let me learn the craft
of you, bob your craft
on the high thigh seas,
seed the beads of sweat
into garments of pearls, pearl
your hair into ribbons, bows
of dredlocks and curls, craft
the witty lines into stories
of release: the crafty ties,
sweet meat rubbing, mind rubbed
portrait of you on my
pillow. All the witchcraft fails
to express the spent spells,
fare-thee-wells, the heart
crafted canny of making you
by hand, the molding, smoothing
your heartwood chest, my legs
linking to your burl and
dowel. Our fine art printing,
darkroom beginning—our heavenly craft.

Loving you takes some resourcefulness,
a picking up of sticks
and stones, the crumbling bones
of an imagined future. If
I were to love you
I would leave myself behind,
hide away in my nutshell
of cowering, re-membering, the long
night of some new beginning.
I gather my resources, my
humble-pie, my few fallen feathers,
the expression I glean from
rocks or the heart's river.
I could flow with you
no more. I've come to
the confluence of breaker and
bar, resourceful as Friday, clammed
up in my shell of silence.
I'm standing on some island.
Re: source: resorting, resourcing; outsourced.

What I love about you
goes beyond your Latitudinarian attitude.
It's in the feathers you
pray on, the wind in
your sage, the amber copal
of your eyes, red cedar
smoke you use to speak
to the ancestors. I love
the trail of tears in
your history you carry between
your eyes, that book of
laughter and forgetting you read
to me at night. It's
in your hands with their
smudged knuckles, the old remnants
of the blows there, the
fist of your heart beating
in a gentler time. I
love the ruleless you, the
me I find in you.

Please please me, sang Paul,
and I believed. I do
please you, please the nape
and the pillow of your
chest. Pleasure fluffs a supple
spine, twines mine and twins
us. Over and over again
the same passage, same song
of spent passion (an investment
in our future.) Pleas for
subtlety escape us as we
come into that great escape.
I'll be the valve, you
be the intake, and this
engine of the heart revs
its pleasing octaves. Oil me
shining and, please, please me.
Make me purr on the
road to our tomorrow. Just
pleasure and pleasant and pleasing.

Loving you takes some restraint,
takes time, takes a line
of well-wishers in the wings,
takes a wing and being
there, takes care. I wouldn't
want to be your leash
and call, your water bowl,
your long time left in
the sun. Loving you takes
some restraint, some straining, panting
in the missing you part.
Loving you ought not be
heavy rain in the arroyo
or a flood of nightmares.
I don't want to choke
in an overgrown garden, fat
blooms of potential nettles all
around us: a stinging cure
for stiffening; a healing brew,
not out of control; recovery.

How did I ever wind
up with this? What wind
put this house down with
this inside it? What winding
road led me to this
rocky path? What raw wind,
what sand blasted away this
statue with it? This pillar
of salt looks on: dry
plains of ash, wet clay
feet in a pile, my one
wind up doll exhausted in
the wake. On a windy
day, all day, the silent
pushing, heaving, the winding spiral
of leaves tightening, a gyre,
a wound up wire of
fishline emptying into the invisible
wind. This winding down, wan,
winsome final smile, this wind.

II.

We were babes in Toyland,
two, set for the hearth;
two, but for the plot.
The villain was our own.
Possibly. Time, bent on kidnap—
always a dark forest, foraging,
the great escape. Never enough
toys to appease him, villain
clocks in their towers chime.
One? Two? You, finally falling
for me, Mary Quite Contrary.
Even the perfect couple must
suffer the slings and arrows,
dressed well for the part,
heart in hand, a sleeve
for the sheep, safely stolen,
on greener fields. I light
upon the part where you're
sold to a gypsy band;
I play it to heart.

Come back home to that
grotto we make in the
dark, to the still water
still pooling and deepening; there,
where we recess to gill
and fin; there, where even
our breaths relive their pasts.
I want you in the
crevice of my heart, a
recirculation, recycling touch, wearing, lapping
horizon as we lay it
down forever in a day.
Sleepy grotto of undulating waves;
you, oyster to my pearl.
I glisten you to morning;
but in the flesh—you
are gone. An empty spot
pours out its art upon
the page—imagining you there:
salt, spray, wind weeping sea.

If 100 words is all
it takes to write me
back to you, I say,
bring on the fractures, new
fissures, the tiny breaks in
the heart, all the on
and off in the mathematics
of we two—wee bits
of light catching the fold.
I say, say it simple,
keep it close to chest.
One switch puts it all
in play—this television drama
splicing us together or apart.
I say, this spring season
watch all the episodes with
me. Dance across the screen.
Let me knead you to
your final conclusion. Let's laugh,
a fractal imagining, and love.

I want to be pixilated,
twitterpated by you. I want
to be rounded up and
eaten—drunk on the expressed
hunger of your mess. Buy
me 100 ways into your
heart, Sell me 100 tickets
to your whole lotto love.
I want to stay for
the whole show, chew up
the scenery, dance on the
dinner plates. I see pixies
in your eyes, your sensuous
lips. I want to wade
too far into the current.
Certified; and surrendered; I want
to watch as my body
drifts too far out in
the throes, to live in
you, close to the heart.

Baby, let me twist your
tube. Let me dial you
up a new dimension. Let
me see you in one
thousand lights. Let me eye
you into infinity. Let your
lips and legs go akimbo.
Give all your smallest bits
to me. Let me gaze
through you into your he-art,
into the many factors, into
the paradise of your multiple
rainbows. Each color, another note
in the inner song. Each
fine slice of you served
up on a spinning plate.
Let me handle your changes,
ride past your infinite divisions.
Let me turn you around.
Help me see through you.

R-E-S-P-E-C-T
I found out what
it meant to me.
R-E-S-P-E-C-T
to be the breath of
me—*for a little respect.*
Just a little bit. Just
a little bit more on
your lips, your wit, your
used up heart. I finger
the loose tooth absence: you
missing from my art, my
Valentine picture of us now
folded in two with you
under the fold. I'm trying
again. To catch the wind
under my wing, to sail
on off to the continent
of my contentment, to name
all my unknown dreams and
land one, one sweet succulent
place where I stand, alone.

I want to be there
at that exact moment when
you know you love me,
when you feel that waterfall
down your spine and into
your solar plexus, when winds
of change change you and
your smile sails ships of
its own. I want to
be there when you discover
me: a deserted island of
your own making, when summer
recovers our skin, a soft
pelt dissolving upon contact, when
all the ice of other
touches melt upon our heat
and all the rivers in
our veins open up in
utter awe of it. I'll
be there, exactly, totally. There.

Christopher Robin would know what
to do. With a man
like you, I'd have to
put on my thinking cap.

You are so far away
and not a holiday travel.
You are distant as Skull
Island, distant as a tree
in the 100 Acre Wood.

Purely imaginaire. I think, therefore
I am. Here, in my
wooden stump, the well swept
heart bares not a crumb.
Where is your honey pot?

Where is your far away
look? I make a beeline
for your eyes, those lips,
that crusted mind. Grumpy as
Eeyore, is that my cloud?

Are you my tail? Love?

You were meant for me.
The rest is just poverty,
a piss poor way home,
a basket of backyard oranges,
fat potatoes, too many eggs.

You were born for me,
born to the loser's class,
born to sorrow, born full
of all that you've been
missing, born half-way there.

You were waiting for me,
waiting to eat your fill,
waiting out tomorrow, a future
tense, a perfect reunion: you,
last splash in the present.

You were once my destiny, my
one-way ticket out of poverty,
a full tank of gas,
a brimming goblet, a lotto
love for you—for me.

I'm not afraid of poverty.
I have your golden touch.
I have your threadlike hair.
I have the gold coin
and gentle rain of you.

I'm not afraid of poverty.
I could sip your soup
all day. I would play
with your remains, twist you
into endless mouthfuls, love you.

I'm not afraid of poverty,
not with this filling music,
not with these eyes, lips
that could cradle a tongue,
all that lean of you.

I'm not afraid of poverty.
I have your meaty heart.
I have the best of you.
I have your art
of loving back, have you.

You show me no mercy,
have me wearing Pablo's cape,

going about the sorrow-sucked streets
singing to myself, searching locked

faces for calla lilies like
a dog with an egg

in her mouth. You want
roses? Nights in love with

the bloom in your hand?
Give me tough seeds, plants

that grow only in deserts,
trees that sprout through fire.

I want you, your expressed
desire, olive oil from your

sultry secrets, salty taste of
your memories, what doesn't live

tomorrow but in the eternal
today of your sudden loving

smile. You made me me.
You! Show me no mercy!

Baby, let me blog you.
Lemme lay down the law
of you. I'll express you
and expedite your better half.
I'll succumb to the expression
of your essential all, your
many traces, those love sounds
only I can hear. Here
I'm blogging away on a
dream and a scheme, some
springtime thing when a fling
ain't enough. I want your
inner secretions, those mysteries
of you. I won't tell,
only sketch your outline on
the page. At this stage
I want to blog you,
log-in to you, upload your
downloads, test out your hardrive:
your inner desire for me.

What a sweet scandal, you
and I: the parrot and
the butterfly. Sweet-faced alibi,
salami to my denim, you
are the irrepressible me. Your
eyes: twin cenotes in this
remembered garden, a past exploit.
What scandal, you and I,
if pride could lie. If
I could tick it backwards,
live life like an Iowa
election machine, would I reveal
the outcome? Would I lie
between your forest thighs? Would
I try? Be a kite expressing,
pulling at the knot? I'm
all over you in a
sigh. I'm the sign of
you, an image in light—
your scandalous sight; strobe: you.

Walk with me. I want
to wet your feet in
a field of a million
wild iris, our willing hearts
as rare as that, a
loving mass under the earth,
there among the worms and
crystals. Purple blushing into pink
for the bee. Our buzz
at the reeling touch. I
want you, at the foot
of my mile, my miracle
of you stunning over bog,
a zillion blades of green
glee over the murky bottom.
You, your feet in mud,
the clay of you melting
into me after the fact,
I want you, your feet,
your act. Step to me.

I saw you in the ocean,
the irrepressible you, the you
I couldn't keep out. On
those wet wings, the waves
lapping at my shoulders, I
fantasized my way into life,
into my life here, bloom
to the sturdy stem, rose
to the salve, imagining summer,
energetic springs with you, dogs
swimming in the surf. I saw
you in the way water
hurls itself into the air
like a whale breaching, lilacs
spewing a stream of floral
spray in the sea-foam waiting
there—on the weighty wings
of the dead—expressed there
in the ocean, a winged
prayer, a surge, some stay.

Verde, que te quiero verde.
— Federico García Lorca

Blood that I love you.
Blood that I take you.
Blood that lets the lying
dog lie. Blood that lets.
Blood that lets in. Blood
that I give you, real
blood from my veins. Blood
that I see you. Blood
offerings in the sky. Blood
like a cloud of dust
in your sky, some crystallization
of the diamond you. Blood
that took you. Blood that
vampire. Blood the assassin. Blood
betrayer. Blood belittler. Blood
the betrothed. Blood that takes
you away from me before
you even are. Blood relative
to the ocean of your
heart—your art in blood.

I want to distill you
down to your final essence,
strain you through the tight
sieve of my sense, through
the thighs and the back
40 where I lie and
you wait, fermented and fine.
I want to age you
to a mellow sparkle, woo
you with wisps of whiskey
and rye (wry little drops
left on flask.) I want
you any way I can
get you. I don't want
you to bottle up your
heartwood or explode into spontaneous
flame. I want you charmed
and tendered, heated and biting
ever so slightly. I want
your liquor, your oozing, you!

100 words for my ass.
You want the upward pass,
a long stream of vowels,
some sweaty consonants, my perky
verbs, 100 breathy fricatives. You
express me more than move
me. Olive oil in my
roe—a smooth slide to
indecision, a lithesome ride for
two. 100 words for just
my ass. How many words
for the view? How many
acts of you will it
take before this woman sings,
before the ring of you?
100 words for my ass.
Worth a quarter or two,
my peach, my apple half.
What would you give to
join the rest of few?

I look at you, poser,
and who else would I
do? You who are back
at arm's length, a pixel
away, a continent. I would
develop, it's true, an inkling
of you, a shadowed outline,
a rule. I am always
looking up at you, hanging
on the lank of you.
I want the action you,
the back-shot you, the guttural
felling you. I come back
like a grunion, flashing my
belly for you, a poser, too,
a healer, a looker—appealing
to you to take off
that frown, strip down to
your smile and ground, that
terra firma of you. Illustrious.

Grief makes a family. Every
death takes us further from
ourselves, out where the dust
forms into galaxies, matrices of
trust—the threads we tuck
under time, the taking time
to tuck or cover. My
time with you: an embroidered
shawl, a magnifying glass, a
glass of water. Too brief.
So long. Old friend. Amigo
del camino del sól. Critic
to the end. Suavecito muy
lindo. El sueño de mí,
sígue. Criticando. Signifying. Clarifying. Refining.
My life is half-empty
without you—music without the
chair, plate missing the meal,
this family of you without
you grieving songs of you.

III.

I want your fire, not
your flame, what cauterizes, what
heals, what enriches the soil.
I want the fire of
you, what burns fine to
touch, what blazes in your
gaze, the St. Elmo's Fire
of your dreaming, the ashes
of your mea culpas. I
want what evaporates hot tears,
what transforms doubt into must.
I want the sudden lick,
the gulp of magic, tasseled
sunsets all around. I want
the molten core, the dynamo
between your thighs, cauldron inside
your eyes. Alchemized. I want
the wisest you, the wizen
you, word wizard you, enchanting,
bolt of spell—of you.

What would it take to
kiss? A plane trip? A new
outfit? Benign weaponry? Silken parachute?
Box of coal as consolation?

What will it take to
kiss that smile that breaks
at your guarded silo's shore?
What will it take to

kiss words off—type my
signature across your chest, crush
in fur, bathe in life-sweat
and substance? What word will

it take to silence words,
that duck and cover of
the heart? Kiss and lie
in your imagined earth, kissing

your matter from the maw?
Let me put my lips
to your fire. Surround your
words for the final surrender.

You wear your mystery well.
To look at you, one
would never guess. Tucked inside,
a note in my pocket,
a gleam in your inner
eye—Who would have thought
you would light me like
this? Caught by the half-light
of your budding smile, your
starry lines, an intense setting
subjunctive. There's something going on.
It's a mystery to me,
a great story told by
fire, a heartful drop in
the bucket. Every page, another
clue, another twist in the
plot-lines, another morsel of you
on the path we make
as we move, another destination
toward you; way up, out.

100 words is all it
takes to get you to
notice me noticing you notice
me. 100 words is all
it took for me to
notice you, notice the novel
in your shadowed eyes, the
twinned stanzas of your fine
hands, the miracle of your
secret heart. 100 words, all
it took for me to
want the art of you,
the watercolor of the night
with you, the hidden waters
of your singular river, want
the lure along with your
hook, your lead, your sinker.
I want the living rhythm
of you, the mundane day
of you in your notice.

You are so fine. I
finally see it. Fine, fine
me. Tell me how to
pay: for the luxury of
luxuriating under your gaze, for
lengthening the gap between me
and any others, for nuzzling
my way back into some
core, for the fine fur
on your head, your buck
and saddle. You, the finest
you in you. And I
at the shore, the fine
earth all under your waters.
To be under you, I
would give all the finest
horses - with you, under you,
I would ride the fine
typology, your open set. My
fine. I would be fine.

I hope to be the
brown earth to your many
rivers, a deepening cenote to
what pools within, the fourth
ventricle, the missing flap to
your heart. I hope to
be many spirits inside you,
four on the floor to
your get up and go.
I hope to be what
fuels you, what fills you
up, what whets. I hope
to be luminous to your
touch, an opalescent fire that
never burns but cauterizes your
cicatrices, your fortuna, your proud flesh
over the pumping force; hope
to be your you
for you, your fourth dimension.
I hope to be your hope.

I am ripening, a part
of your tree, this sudden
graft. I am leaning towards
what brightens me, eternal, fine.
I am opening the heart
of this pit, this healing.
For you. For the strange
taste of a summer stranger,
lure of the allure, this
sweetening, I am ripening past
and into desire; this unleaving,
this simple bursting, this noticeable
creep towards harvest. I am
all color and juice, tarty
flavor, the cumulation of my
youth. For you, my sun,
my tender, my multiple meanings.
For the many things you
may do with this body
of work. For your release.

Baby, you are the nail.
Let me be the hammer.
Cleave to me, be filling
for the hole without you.
You nail it every time:
your words, your voice, that
look. Too easy, it was,
to nail me, I know.
All it took was your
angels touch, those key pads
under your nails fretting
my back, there. I wanted
you from first glance, first
read—how you hit it
on the head. Now, in
your bed, the luxurious length
of you beside me, now
I get the point. Come
and nail me. Kiss me.
Keep me on your cross.

Splendid, you are, in your
lair. Splendid in your hair,
the fuzz cut and fur
there. Splendid, you are, between
bare thighs, the rise under
the ridge, that splendid fig.
You were such a figment
of my intent, My Fish,
My Snare, My One that's
Not Away—though I dare
to call you there; splendid
in your full extension; my
own sure cure for love-
soldiering, sole hunting in valleys
of loneliness, rallying through songs
and flowers (not as splendid
as you.) Splendid in your
honesty of a nail, truthful
as bark. Love, the splendid
cat splay of you. Basking.

I want to render you
a rock, be hard in
the stay, firm you up
not grind you down. I
don't want to mold you.
I want to form you
through steady use. I don't
want to bust you up
just because I know I
can. I want you whole,
the whole of you inside.
I want your seedy kernel,
the sand of your time.
I want to find you
here, like a carved crystal,
(your single tongue tolling my
bell), pearl to my oyster,
rock to my soft place.
I want to rock you,
pick you up, keep you.

(an elegy)

How much hope we had.
Restraint was how we grew.
Ever twining our long way
out of there; intertwining sans
desire. You, a golden Lotus,
Darling. (How you fit that
warm shoe: *Darling*.) You wore
that new car scent, crisp
and sweet, succulent, for a
man. Did I covet you?
Like the rest. I shouldered
my restraint. Strapped into you,
how could I escape? That
ejection seat. This far from
you, without restraint, I'll say
it, how I loved you.
How death did us part.
You were my heart. Devéras,
Carnál, Corazón, and at last.
We gave us our past.

I so needed a change.
Rats had got my past.
The future, a dim wheel
egging me on until rooster.
This heart was a chicken
with her head cut off.

All along, you, my grunion,
ensconced in your sea of
mud, orders and revisions were
raiding your larder of dreams,
dreaming of the next pantry
of goods, another nightshift alive.

How I wanted a change
and changed because of it;
changed into changeling (maybe lonely
for discovery), all my relations
scattered on wing and smoky
prayers (every word, a prayer).

Changed by you. For you.
Loose change in your pocket.

I was ready to receive
you, embrace you, take you
into me. Receive. Could it
be you were onto me?
Were you receiving this song?
Like an old favorite you
entered my dreams, the reception
flickering until your signal comes
strong. Would you receive me
if I skipped a beat,
if I turn it up
full blast? I want you
into me. I want you.
I was an empty reception
hall, a plate with no
food. I was a quartz
tube until you fit this
socket. I was an overloaded
extension cord, a fused copper
wire, exposed; until your connection.

You're better than a vibrator,
Baby, better than a double
mocha, better than this stupid
love song on the radio,
better than a flash fiction
of desire, better than moon,
better than the vibes I
get from the tide of
you rising inside me. This
vibration of you so attuned
to whatever. Vibrating under your
thighs like the tribal bracelet
still embedded in your wrist,
like a calling in your
pocket, like leaves just before
that final letting go, Baby,
you're just better than a
vibrator, how you've got those
other speeds sending me into
good vibrations, vibrating to you.

Baby, you don't need Money.
You need me, my siren
in the surf, my song
in the dawn for you.
Who needs Money? Anyone's got
Money. Ah, but who you
are, your inner change, that
spare coinage when you speak,
the enchanted gold of your
tongue—and its place! Baby,
who needs Money? You've got
a gal like me, even
for a bargain. You, my
blue light special: with those
raptor eyes, lackadaisical sighs, wise
assed smiles in the comments;
every hundred dollars in your
heartbeat, that shirtful of soul;
Baby, who puts a price
on a heart like that?

I'm quiet in the muse
of you, quiet in the
stand of you, your root,
your laden arms. I'm quiet
after the fruit of you,
quiet in the sate of
you. Satisfied. I'm satisfied with
you. I get that satisfaction.
Come and service your station.
Now that I'm tuned into
you and fine tuned to
your purr and engine's growl,
I'm quietly waiting for you,
waiting for your automatic shift
and slip. I'm holding fort.
I'm holding on to you,
holding fast to my gas;
and steady. I'm quietly musing,
resting in your field (transplanted),
on neutral, satisfied at last.

You've got me all provocative,
Babe. You've got me bearing
my assets. Witness my will
with you, flash and sass.
You've got me baring
arms, my ridges, my valleys,
my sweetened avenues,
exquisite private views,
waiting for you to collect
your first term sweat equity.

Honey, come and see what
you do to me. How you
fit the honeyed slip, slit
through with you I'm leaking
dreams, whetting to your hone.
Hanging on my phone,
you move me to provoke.
Your provocation keeps me up
all night. Baby, let me
provoke you while I'm waiting
for your poke. What provocation!

I have this perception. You
are who you are, been
where you've been. I know.

I know what anyone knows
short of nothing. I know
birds return (not to me.)

I know what I feel,
what hurts, the shape of
you on top of me.

Perception, like me, once extinct,
now, an insurrection of knowledge.
Now, I percolate through dreams.

You dream me into cloth,
into your warmth beside you.
Whatever sign do I need?

So plainly, snow-tracks, fallen
cake crumbs for you, messages
that pass through mountains, pass

through diamond and mist: waves
of missing you, particle's change.

All the world's a street.
Come and celebrate. Walk with
me. March to the heart's
syncopation. The cacophony of mindless
pigeons, the jangle in half-empty
pockets—all a forgotten melody.
Just change. Dance with me.
Fall into this celebration of
you. Let the shredded confetti
of past mortgage coupons, bus
passes, what you get from
the pumps fill up your
avenues. Lighten your loaded questions,
canons of information, study exams.
It's all a celebration, all
gravy from here on out.
Treat it like a won
election. An win, win paradise.
Our mariachis of mornings, waiting
under oompahs and streetlights, dawn.

There is the fragmented you,
mosaic you, that face you
shave, that fine fur covering
your stone: military you, savior
you; you, tucked fertile bug
in a log cut up
for firewood; shattered state you,
beginning again you, resourceful you,
the you I swim inside,
the you I hide in
the heart of me—one
bittersweet chocolate, you inside my
books, you off the hook;
you, breathing into me; You
are fragmented into a rainbow
way, prismed for play—warrior
you, you in the field, a
you so rare its worth
is valueless. Valuable to
me. Just you. For me.

IV.

Here I come to you
with this woolen heart, this
furball heart; heart, my squashed
acorn. I come here seducing
you, weighing you to my
gold: felt passages, lugubrious basking,
mesmerized asp in my basket.
Come to me, my willing
carrier. Come and stroke my
nap, curry the knap—this
hip, this lip—rub the
purr from my belly. A
raging fire waits inside this
hearth set for you. Here
where I'm blessed with your
imagined flank, close enough for
scent, I insist you into being:
shell to my hollow, Heart-
felt Stranger reduced by heat
to my bristle and mink.

You were on my wavelength,
baby; so short was your
temper—that gamma ray you,
that in the flesh annihilating
you—that all the sun
tomorrow couldn't make up for
your implosion. Your past explosions,
something lodged in the chest,
all the fallout: I know.
How slow. I didn't notice
the small alterations, tiny tears
in the proximity of you.
Laser beam you / gamma knife
you, how you laid me
open for surgery. Penetrating you,
finding all of my gaps.
Medicine you, irradiating you, turning
my topaz heart to blue.
Gamma ray you, how I
loved, Love, in your orbit.

Worse than rage, you stole
my love poem to give
to another woman, changed my
line to the "Aurora Borealis"
(her classical composition.) *Not too
classy,* my last words to
you. You who would always
speak without being spoken to,
who never shut up, I
never loved you. Here's 100
words about your Aurora Borealis:
an illusion left by heat.
Now, I'll temper a man
earthy as grit, fragile slate,
more than your slag, one
who's unafraid of the silence
we speak. I'll make up
for you in the bird
sounds I make: night words
you will never hear. Closer.

I'm thankful for your breath,
Today I'm thankful for our
death—so far from us
today, but informative, a sacred
trust. I'm thankful for my
life of getting to know
your life, of moving ahead
to touch. I'm grateful for
the steps you take through
another season, for sensuous leanings
toward another winter. I thank
the trees, their whispers through
our lungs. I thank our
separate seas, the gentle lapping
of our thighs. I thank
you, your fire and clay.
I take Thanksgiving in your
smile. I feast my way
through the cornucopia of you
so thankful for the right.

Waiting, yes, I'm waiting. I'm
just here waiting for you.
I'm waiting for the end
of the world's desire, waiting
for the planetary shift in
the heart to occur, waiting
for the upset of the
century. I wait for birds
to find their way home,
wait for you to open,
radiant and full of yourself,
helping yourself to my nest.
I am waiting for summer
to subsist or submit, resisting
the change of the season's
guard. I am waiting for
you in your glory, you
in the hoary frost warming
your nature on my breast
and wing—waiting for me.

I couldn't see the moon
last night as it approached
perigee, but I heard it
all night in the sea's
lustful cries, the splashing crash
of the earth's desire, felt
it throw itself at the
land: a fantasy of loose
spray, an act of passion.
What I couldn't see filled
me, a kind of feathered
hope, a way of waving
off this waiting, this sudden
aging, moon-shift. All night
the lit cranking, the bucket
of the world going up
without me. Holding on to
all her nothing, her radiant
rays, the rags of her
aura, bléssed upon the ocean.

In this queer weather all
bets are off. Winter won't
comply. Fall has already disrobed.
The thin sheaves of summer
flake off in my hand.

And what are we to
make of Spring? Her smock
of cherry plum petals, her
greenly asphodels wait for the
seed to fall. All blown.

In this queer weather all
hands raise into the air
feeling for dew, and do
fall back, a subtle back
stroke across a cloud sea.

And a cumulus accumulates, us
in another day, mouths entangled,
words evaporating into rain. Storm
warning breaks into calm blue,
the queerest, passing into you.

Walk with me, and we'll try
to illuminate the sky. Why
wouldn't the weather comply? We've
got a bridge to the
heart. You have an art
of drawing me out. You
have those artful hands, those
soulful sighs: your eyes, cosmic
dust of which I am
just a particle. I don't
care one iota for your
past. You are a gas
and I am the energy
source through the tube. You
strobe me on unto some
kind of Delaware of Venus.
The circumference of your smile
captured in filament and glass.
All you have to do
is illuminate me with you.

Just 100 words of goodbye
this first day, taken. This
first new year, extravagant in
its pleasure of red, its
greenly hills, its winding down.

It's winding down to you
and past. Past the warmth
of your shoulder, your stroke,
past the filigree of smiling
eyes, your strong-arm rung.

I'm writing 100 words for
goodbye. I'm staying on in
my future—not a perfect
tense. I'm holding on to
the pluperfect past of you.

I'm addressing your finest nature.
I'm appealing to the head
of your heart. I am breaking
some pact of independence,
some right to bear arms.

It's true, you stimulate me.
And it's good that you
do, good that the well
comes to the bucket, good

that you're a salmon swimming
upstream, good that when you
rain everything comes up green
in me. It's true. Beauty

dons an hundred veils. Your
beauty is a kiss away.
Come and taste the true
in me. Dive into tomorrow.

All we are is water
and the cleverest salt, all
we feel is something squared:
a voice in the ear,

64k. Someday, this will all
be yours: my lips on
your neck, going up into
paradise, stimulating the inner you.

Here's a vignette: a man
is typing into a woman's
life. He's eating up her
heart with every pixel served.
He's an economy unto himself.
She is very soft, softest
skin in the West. He's
Eastern bred, a New jersey
field of wild passion lilies.
The rest is underground and
under-said. The rest is rest.
They are resting until their
futures rise up with blank
vengeance, with pleasure, with sex
in the bank; two banks
holding, a levee unto themselves.
Until they are lovers they
will never be apart. Imagined
until flesh, they are opening
the vined gate: me, you.

I won't be your Muse, Baby.
I'll be your amusement for hours.
I won't be your finery, Baby.
I'll be your nugget of fire.
I won't be your desire, Baby.
I'll be your heartstone for life.

The rarity of you, the fused texture
that heats to your skin of me.
Baby, we make the geode, rife
and rift, we are quartz and sandstone melded
in the power of love—to risk the rather
quaint. You pause me in the telling
exploration of you—a lump of
kerfuffle left in a box, this ordinary
mystery, collision of worlds
leaves me kerfuffle.

Love with you is impossible;
Impossible with any you you
are; impossible in the filtration,
the clarification, the gradation. You,
my select grade-a, my single
egg in which I am
not the twinned yolk, I
would have loved you unto
the next day, into a
morning that finds me tending
your flowers. We could have
been more than maybe, more
than a handful, more than
the fired seed I am,
more than what's left over
from the flood of you.
I could have been more
than your faucet, wet in
the after-dew—more than me
in the why of you.

Baby, I want a repeat
performance. I want you up
on the wire. Baby, I'll
pay my admission to you
again: the steamy matinees, full
orchestra to accompany the reels.
I want another encore, Baby,
want you on my world.
Let's stage that love scene
once again. Let's do all
our own action shots. You
got me on repeat dial.
Call me to the rehearsal.
Let me fill in, stand-in.
Let me be your standby
stand again. Let me be
your oozy mass. Re-peat me,
baby, now that I'm bogged,
down for not getting down
with you. Take me. Repeat.

You. Devastatingly you, you are
so you in your youness
I would recognize you anywhere,
wherever you are, my uncovering
tomb, my unnailed raider, my
next wave in the chute,
I am coming to you.
I am nothing more than
distance and syrup, vocals and
ash. Come to me as
you are: deep in my
breath-house, coveted as honey and
gas. Explore with me, our
inner nature. Be one with
this mountain of you. Smell
my hair, let it lead
you to some remainder of
home: a keen and silver
place above the surf, anchored
in reef, coral and you.

Loving you is pure genius,
smartest thing I've ever done.
It's the "O" in my
mega, the alpha to this
end. It's Robert Johnson playing
my heart, but lower. Loving
you explains it all: my
unified field, my saliva strings
between the knees; my drool
over you, a Jackson Pollock
expression. Loving you is genius:
Hans Bethe refusing to make
the neutron bomb, Star Wars, fake
suns in some other world
of us. It's the noblest
prize I'll ever win, shining
as I come to know
you, rust-free. Loving you
is quantum mechanics made simple,
is charmed and quarky: you!

Man, I want you noisy,
noisy as a room full
of squonking saxophones, noisier than
a bagpipe convention in Glasgow.
I want you to make
some noise for me, because
of me. I want you
pealing and babbling in tongues.
I want to toll you
as I roll you, sound
test you and check your
mic. Baby, I want to
crank it up to 100.
I want us to keep
the cats up all night.
I want your heart on
a Marshall amp. I want
to bear all the Bose
of you down to bone.
Let me hear your love!

I know you thought we
were toast, thought I'd burned
our love away. "I thought
I was toast," you said.
But I could still eat
your heart everyday every way
a heart could get eaten.
I want you back. I
want you on my plate.
I want your blue light
special. I want every day
of you, every last crumb.
I want your silly feet.
I want the metal oozing
past your pores. I'll burn
through your nightmares, leave you
a dream you can remember.
I want to toast to
our longevity. I want toast,
cake. I'll eat it, too.

Around you all is unfolding.
Dramatic petals of your heart
unfold. All is hands, unclasping.
The warmth of you, unfurling
fire to my log, flame
to my tongue. Let me
raise your flag. Hoist your
moist mouth onto my unfolded
glistening. Be the sweat rolling
down my downy opening. Be
the bee pestering to honey,
dew on the unrumpling finery.
Be these coverings. The wool
of you, unwrapped between nipples.
All your splayed out limbs
limbering my spine. My fine
explosions, unfolding origami over you.
Licking the flap, your lips,
your you over me. Let
me be your heart unfolding!

There is no way, Baby,
no compass for this desire,
no easy way to you,
no map for the unfolding.

There is no way, Baby.
This heart draws a circle
straight to your bull's-eye, caught
in your lasso: you tame.

But there's no way, Baby,
no charting this wilderness, your
rambling brambles, sloughs, exquisite topography
off the charts, your circumference.

Ain't no way, no way,
Baby. This love is its
own GPS, its own radar,
own sonar: our intermittent wail.

Let me lap your way-out
West, invade your Middle East.
Where there's a will there's
a way, Love, to you.

It's not that I aspire
to you, your grace; nor
live with hope you'll come
down and around to me.

I don't aspire to material
favors, don't savor the drink
and spiel, don't suck in
the ravers. Man, I want

you, blood and sweat, no
lunatic nights, no slow-mo waltz
back home. I want your
inner habitat, not your pointed

spire. I want what is
left of you, after hunt,
the breadth of you, your
dearth. I want what matter

can't have: your inner warmth,
beachy Basque musician's smile. Exile's
Son, not my savior, I
aspire to bask in you.

I wonder at the synchronicity
of you, at the planetary
shift that shot your face
into view (those eyes, those
stars.) I wonder at sweet
synchronicities, when our fingers finally
weave, when I take your
hand into mine and lead
it down there. I want
you to take me there,
there where I'll never escape
this timing. I will wait
until flax and cherries erupt,
until the full flower of
you explodes into kingdom come.
I will want the wait
until the heart finds its
place and your chest meets
mine in the embrace and
the slick coincidence of you.

I would never tether you,
string your ball to pole.
I want you to roll,
endless as a good wheel.
I want you sharp, not
deflated, underrated, grated in the
exasperation, desperation of the age.

I would never tether you.
I'd cut the ties and
let us rise; this disguise
of independence sheds its warm
silk and sweat: this weave.

If you tether me, I
would be your kite, your
love, aloft, delighted in lifting.

Let me get a rise
out of you. Smile. Sweet
tension pulls us into destiny,
into our setting sun. We're
falling, we're two wings, folded.

Let me judge the content
of your character, Baby. Let's
open the doors of the
Fridge. I want to see
what you keep in there,
what slays you, what keeps
you lean. Reveal those contents
stripped of context. I want
what's left of your inner
thigh, content to ride you
high and dry. I want
your seldom told stories, your
contentious lines, your soft folds
within the hard surprises. You
shake me. Squeeze it out
of tundra. All is cornucopia.
All is feed and slurp.
Content with the wondrous contents
of your content: Come. Come,
content, and contend with me.

Your body is the only clock
that makes me arrive on time.
— Adrian Arias

You can be my organ
donor. Baby, put your trust
in me. You can sign
away your heart. You won't
feel it when you're gone.
You could fill my bill,
not like any old Dick
and Hairy. You could fit
so succulently this empty chest,
your heart on my breast
above the nipple. That's so
right where you put it.
That organ grinder's monkey dancing
in me wants it all
down to the last tick
tock. Your body, the only
clock that wakes me;
Could I reject that?

You ask if I could
adapt. I could fit like
an oyster: all that suck
excess, that tidal success, skin
inside the wound of miracle.

All of everything learned
to adapt: the frog calling
to the meadow of one,
the single migratory butterfly pumping
in the pursuit of happiness.

Everything adapts. I, to this
joyful nada. You, to these
acres of ghosts, the shot
story, the grande flambé. Let
me be your singing bird.

What you observe, your destiny,
I could adapt to that.
let me option you for
your adaptation. Everything is art
of change. We do, adapt.

You bring out the child
in me, the wild in
me, the not so mild
in me. In you, I
am older than spring, wiser
than the twisted buds. Childlike
and hungry, I look to
you, my tamer, my big
cat stalking the laden heart.
Let me play with you,
stay with you, delay the
inevitable with you, here in
this never-never. You bring
out the childhood joy. Childish
and coy, I will have
you and know—what lucid
children know: that the heart
holds only what it can
carry, that miracles do happen,
that children's ways do pay.

Life without you is chaos,
is all white noise in
the grey matter, a matter
of multiple angles at once.

I can never know what
to expect without you: chaos
in the kitchen, in my
deepest attics, in the closets

where I can expect you
not to be hidden. Hidden
in these rafters, the blueprints
to the foundation of you

don't exist. You are wisps
of my quarky imagination, charmed
particles in flight, what clings
to my core in the

attraction. Any pattern will do.
I do, and long to
lay it on a Fibonacci
sequential spiral dance to you.

It was in the stars.
A falling star foretold you.
Venus was an incoming plane
colliding with Mars and Jupiter,
a single hot eye in
the moonless sky. I wished
for you but never got
on board. Last ticket to
Paradise, a missed opportunity. You
smile, a constellation I use
to find me. Who will
find me? Navigation by heart?
Your dusty trail, a rumor
in the mill of Heaven.
I follow your orbit, circling
you in a cosmic dance.
Hundreds of light years until
tomorrow, until your ghostly touch.
Hundreds of broken hearts before
Venus comes in for landing.

I love all the oddities
of you, the oddball you
with your odd normality, oddest
you as the animal you
can kill with all finality.
You're the oddest love I've
begun to love: oddly fine
and refined as a cat,
cat-licking you, that platinum tongue,
that ravishing you, slow in
your Piscean fun (those fingers!),
the magic in your hands
to soothe, to hold, warm
as a cub in Arctic
heat. I hold you close,
keep you close inside, sheltering
this rara avis I seek,
this skittish roan; this dappled
mare is aware, and grown,
accustomed as yours to own.

It was only a matter
of time before I'd meander
to you. Just time in
its telling wardrobe: the finery
of age and the ages
renewing the contract. I'd contract
with you in order to
expand. Many worlds are possible.
The sea meanders into oceans,
a breath of the babe
meanders into the gaping mouths
of the dead. You resurrect
me, make me want to
meander off the page and
into your idling heart. Let
me kick-start you into
tomorrow. Meander with me. Let
it lead us. Be easy
as the Sunday morning I
first was stunned by you.

I don't mind the grunge
as long as you do
the lunge. Lunch with you
would be sublime. You're my
Michaelangelo. Al fresco, you come
lay it while it's wet.
Grunge with you, Baby, brings
out my inner Patti Smith.
Feeling the knobs above your
thighs, Baby you do it
for me, grunge and all.
Let me scrounge up these
jeans that have seen it
all and I'll try on
you. I'll get by for
you. Me, singing the soil
back in its place, softening
my bed for you—your
place. No matter the race,
Baby, this hare's for you.

What we had is repast,
a mere refection, entremets,
a side-order of side dish.
You made me feel full
of you, your nimble wit
(life with you could've been
a picnic, a teatime dejeuner.)
Now you want to feed
me this ploughman's lunch: cheesy
cracker and a single stalk.
Come on, man, not even
collation! What supper would subsist
of this tiffin? What aliment?
The heart slows when it
sees you on the table.
There'll be small bites tonight,
not much else to nosh
for this dish. In past
our repasts resembled Thanksgiving, all
sit down sweet. Now? Chow.

Beginning with an auspicious number,
three in a row: seven
for "togetherness," you, my lucky
face, my rarest luck, luckiest
number in the west, "arise"
(in Chinese, the male member.)
I associate with you, my
divine divination, my victory over
matter (to some, the perfect
power of the lamb), complete
revelation, my prime, my seventh
ring of Saturn. Come and
fuse this eighth note harmony
as we become fixed as
stars under the twinned orbit
of our spheres. No seventh
son of the seventh son,
I will take you anyway.
Show me the seven paths
to heaven. Auspicious love awaits.

I'm waiting for your google,
Baby, waiting for your probe,
waiting for you to google
me, Baby, waiting for your
spell. I want your fingers
on my mousepad, Baby, your
palm between my pages. Look
me up, I'll be around,
aroused because you're looking. Looka'
here, you'll find me splayed—
all my information. I want
your single click, your sly
exit. I want your google
on my keywords, Baby, your
hand upon my mouse. Interested?
I want you to make
me give it up. I'm
waiting for your hits, waiting
for your stylus, Baby. I'll
lead you here: to us.

Baby, I want you fresh
on me. Your flesh on
me, refreshing as the day
I met you. I want
you to refresh my page,
assuage the rage that's all
around us. I want you
fresh despite your age, your
simmering hope of revival. I'll
revive you, baby, be ice
and fire, compact and just
so salty. I'll try yours,
your catch of the day;
be your late night surprise.
I'll be fresher than suggestive,
just so apropos. I'll be
nature to your city's erection,
top squeeze first thing in
the morning. You'll awake refreshed
to my first charge, daily.

You're so unforgettable. You're so
unregrettably you. I know you're
so gettable. You're so unforgettable
you make statues of men
who graze my glance. You
have that brass, that manner,
that classic stance. You remind
me of no other. You
are sui generis; it's end
of the line for you.
You're so unforgettable. You are
and the world is more
memorable. When you're around you
make all the clues come
true. Yes, you'll do. I'm
sure you'll know when you
want to be; sure you'll
be where you want to
be: right here in front
of me; you, unforgettably you.

I was in a depression.
Fairer weather had flown and
there I was, alone at
the front. A dark cloud
behind me, in the center,
a twisted sunny space, calm
before your storm. I was
that dimple, this life's indent.
I was some tab waiting
for your fill—the order
of you, a calming effect.
You were the lightening strike,
and I, the mixed message,
hot and cold to stark
thought of you, that bank
over the hill. Here I'll
wait, post-depression, when birds
resume their nestings and everything
finds its place. This heart
finds you, alive at last.

I love how you shelter
me, the warmth within your
hearth, all that wood you
had stored. I love all
that wilderness in the heart
of you, all that uncut
lumber just waiting for my
touch. I love the human
path of you, all that
tramping to get there—here
where a river runs through
it, a shelter of smoke,
of sensuous ribbons of past.
Let me demonstrate. I will
lay down my arms, play
dead for you, wait for
your resurrection. Take me. I
know a road clear to
there. It will get us
to where we will last.

At last. Love has come
at last. Last time love
came all it was was
quest. At last, a lasting
love is guest. A visiting
heart came over and, lover,
it's all I'll ever do,
all I can ever see
to win your skipped beat
for me. Consider this plea:
a love you can return
to, a sunny name where
you can, at last, turn
to, and what am I?
But the next stop onto
you. You know you'll do.
At last. My love has
come again. It's been so
long I don't know when—
until I loved you last.

Acknowledgments

"100 Words Against Poverty," "100 Words Past Poverty," and "100 Words For Money" first appeared in The Heretical Consumers Researchers website.

"100 Words Against Poverty," and "100 Words Past Poverty" also appeared in the Triptych Readings website.

"100 Words Over How I Don't Bear A Grudge For The Heart" first appeared in the Online Floricanto of Poets Responding to SB 1070 on La Bloga website.

"100 Words to Spirit" and "100 Words for Wind" forthcoming in *Ariel*, edited by Paul Martínez Pompa, Triton College, 2011.

"100 Words to Radiant," "100 words Over How I Don't Bear a Grudge For the Heart," "100 Splendid Words For the Loneliness Without You," "100 Words to a Noisy You" and "100 Words to the Oddities of You" forthcoming in *No Tell Motel,* edited by Reb Livingston, 2011.

About the Author

A fifth generation Californian of Mexican and Native American (Chumash) heritage, Lorna Dee Cervantes was a pivotal figure throughout the Chicano literary movement She began publishing the literary journal Mango in 1976. Her small press, also named Mango, was widely admired for its creative designs and for the important voices it brought into print, including Sandra Cisneros, Gary Soto, Luis Omar Salinas, and Alberto Ríos.

Her poetry has appeared in literally hundreds of literary magazines and she has been featured on the cover of *Bloomsbury Review* and other literary journals. Cervantes' first book, *Emplumada* (University of Pittsburgh, 1981), a recipient of the American Book Award, was praised as "a seamless collection of poems that move back and forth between the gulf of desire and possibility." Her second collection, *From the Cables of Genocide: Poems on Love and Hunger* (Arte Público, 1991) was awarded the Patterson Poetry Prize, the poetry prize of the Institute of Latin American Writers, and the Latino Literature Award. In 1995 she received a Lila Wallace-Reader's Digest Writers' Award. After a long silence, Cervantes published *DRIVE: The First Quartet* (Wings Press, 2006), a 300-page collection which won the International Latino Book Award.

Cervantes holds an A.B.D. in the History of Consciousness. Until recently she was an associate professor of English at the University of Colorado in Boulder where she directed the creative writing program. She has received two National Endowment for the Arts poetry fellowships and a Lila Wallace Readers Digest Fellowship. She currently lives in her hometown, San Francisco, California. Lorna Dee invites anyone who is interested to visit her blog at http://lornadice.blogspot.com

Related books available from Wings Press:

Drive: The First Quartet
New Poems 1980-2005
by Lorna Dee Cervantes
2006 • Cloth • 310 pages • $24.95
Also available as an ebook.

Drive: The First Quartet
New Poems 1980-2005
by Lorna Dee Cervantes
2006 • Full leather binding • Mahogany box
100 numbered & signed copies • $250

Stunned Into Being:
Essays on the Poetry of Lorna Dee Cervantes
Edited by Eliza Rodriguez y Gibson, Ph.D.
2011 • Paper • 250 pages • $17.95
Also available as an ebook.

Wings Press was founded in 1975 by Joanie Whitebird and Joseph Lomax, both deceased, as "an informal association of artists and cultural mythologists dedicated to the preservation of the literature of the nation of Texas." Publisher, editor and designer since 1995, Bryce Milligan is honored to carry on and expand that mission to include the finest in American writing—meaning all of the Americas—without commercial considerations clouding the choice to publish or not to publish.

Wings Press publishes multicultural books, chapbooks, and ebooks that, we hope, enlighten the human spirit and enliven the mind. Every person ever associated with Wings has been or is a writer, and we know well that writing is a transformational art form capable of changing the world, primarily by allowing us to glimpse something of each other's souls. Good writing is innovative, insightful, and interesting. But most of all it is honest.

Likewise, Wings Press is committed to treating the planet itself as a partner. Thus the press uses as much recycled material as possible, from the paper on which the books are printed to the boxes in which they are shipped. All inks and papers used meet or exceed United States health and safety requirements.

As Robert Dana wrote in *Against the Grain,* "Small press publishing is personal publishing. In essence, it's a matter of personal vision, personal taste and courage, and personal friendships." Welcome to the Wings Press community of readers.

Colophon

This first edition of *Ciento: 100 100-Word Love Poems*, by Lorna Dee Cervantes, has been printed on 70 pound paper containing fifty percent recycled fiber. Titles have been set in Colonna type, the text is in Adobe Caslon type. The printer's device used throughout is based on a Chumash pictograph in a cave in San Marcos Pass, California. All Wings Press books are designed and produced by Bryce Milligan, publisher and editor. The first ten copies were hand bound by the publisher.

On-line catalogue and ordering:
www.wingspress.com

Wings Press titles are distributed
to the trade by the
Independent Publishers Group
www.ipgbook.com
and in Europe by
www.gazellebookservices.co.uk